# The Bookman and the Realtor

— A MURDER MYSTERY —

*Eighth Book in the Zuma Mystery Series*

JEROME RABOW, PH.D.

ISBN 978-1-956010-18-3 (paperback)
ISBN 978-1-956010-19-0 (digital)

Copyright © 2021 by Jerome Rabow, Ph.D.

All rights reserved. No part of this publication may be reproduced, distributed, or transmitted in any form or by any means, including photocopying, recording, or other electronic or mechanical methods without the prior written permission of the publisher. For permission requests, solicit the publisher via the address below.

Rushmore Press LLC
1 800 460 9188
www.rushmorepress.com

Printed in the United States of America

# TABLE OF CONTENTS

Chapter 1:   A Million Dollar Prize.........................5
Chapter 2:   An Expensive Bargain .........................8
Chapter 3:   A Shooter and a Boyfriend ..................12
Chapter 4:   Friends Who Don't Trust....................15
Chapter 5:   The Rich and Famous........................18
Chapter 6:   Sting Like a Bee................................22
Chapter 7:   Who Shall Benefit?.............................24
Chapter 8:   Excellent Liars..................................27
Chapter 9:   The Buyer and the Seller....................29
Chapter 10:  Verifying Authenticity........................32
Chapter 11:  A Strong and Clever Wife...................35
Chapter 12:  Harassment.....................................38
Chapter 13:  Circles............................................40
Chapter 14:  Creating a New Business......................42
Chapter 15:  The Guilty Benefit..............................44
Chapter 16:  George Gershwin...............................46
Chapter 17:  A Dead End......................................48
Chapter 18:  Another Art Collector.........................50
Chapter 19:  Cooperation.....................................52
Chapter 20:  A New Excellent Liar..........................55
Chapter 21:  Dining and Celebrating........................58

# 1

# A Million Dollar Prize

"There is absolutely no need to rush Ms. Henderson. Take a few, slow deep breaths."

Detective Joe Zuma watched the elegantly dressed woman pause. She had come to the precinct and demanded to speak to him, indicated that she admired his work and the way he spoke to the police, the press, and the public. She would speak to no one else but Zuma. The clerk saw that she was a woman who was accustomed to getting her way and to be waited on. He alerted Zuma who told the clerk to let her in.

"Are you ready to speak slowly now Mrs. Henderson?"

"I am. I was in the book store in the mall where I usually purchase books or just browse. A man comes up to strike up a conversation. I don't think he is trying to hit on me. He indicated that he was in the book business but had come to Los Angeles to start his graphic design business.

I tell him I have just bought a new home and ask if he would like to make some sketches of how he would design it. I added that I would be happy to pay him for the sketches. I don't know what made me do this. Maybe it was because he seemed so straightforward and I felt I could help him get started in this new career of his. He said he would be happy to make the sketches and receive payment but also said that if were to use the sketches he would want more money based on the amount of money I was going to spend on the interior."

I told him I would check with my lawyer to see if that was legal. He did not seem happy with that but said that would be OK. I handed him my card, told him the dimensions of my home. I'm in real estate so I know those things. I say goodbye and that I will be getting in touch with him as soon as he sends me his e-mail. As I am standing in line to pay for my books, the same man is asking a woman if he can get ahead of her as he is late for an appointment and if he is late his shrink would want to spend the whole hour talking about lateness. I knew that sounded fishy. How could he have a shrink appointment so soon after arriving in Los Angeles from New York? The woman agrees and when he gets in line and pays for his one book the bell rings. It turns out he is the ten millionth customer to buy a book in Barnes and Noble and will win a million dollars. The woman whom he has gotten ahead of argues but to no avail. I tell the clerk that he asked to get ahead of the woman. The clerk says she can do nothing about it. I told him that what he had done seemed unfair and the least he could do was to offer her half of the prize money. He looked at me like I was nuts. I had regrets about giving him my card. He walked away asking to see the manager so he could claim his prize.

"I'm not sure where this is going, Ms. Henderson. I don't quite see any leave."

"I want you to stop the stalking. He is scaring me."

"Ms. Henderson, it would take a few days for you to fill out a complaint, we would have to locate him and he could delay the process by saying he was just trying to find out if you were going to use his sketches. I have a better idea, if you will go along with it. Why don't I have someone show up at your home in the morning? You can point him out and I can bring him in on charges of harassment."

"I like that idea better but can you be the one who picks him up?"

Zuma saw that she was not going to let go and even though that was much earlier than he started work he thought it would be good relations.

"I'll do that Ms. Henderson but I would also like you to come back to the precinct so the two of you can talk. I don't only want your version. Are you willing to do that?"

"As long as you are the one in the office an. Thank you, Detective. I'll drive my car to your precinct as soon as I see the jerk put in a police car."

# 2

# An Expensive Bargain

Zuma woke up extra early so he could get his morning walk on the Santa Monica beach. He loved watching the sun change the dark sky to light hues 'till it hit the ocean and reflected back. The homeless who had slept on the beach knew him and also knew that he would not bother them. He loved this routine and did it no matter what the weather, even rain. When he got back to take his shower, he saw his wife Claudia had not awakened and had set the alarm for 8:30. He set the coffee machine to start its drip process kissed her gently on the cheek and left for his office in Santa Monica. He felt blessed to have Claudia. He met Claudia four years ago while vacationing in Truro, Massachusetts. There was an instant attraction and passion. Now their relationship was not so much one of passion as it was the amalgamating of two different metals to make something more brilliant. She was a landscape painter and her vistas of Cape Cod with their space and quiet readily spoke to those exact preferences of his. His Pacific was her Cape Cod.

Santa Monica had become the city where actors, directors, agents, and sports stars had bought homes. Unlike East L.A., and the rest of the greater Los Angeles area had air that you could breathe 360 days a year without alerts from the health authorities to stay indoors and avoid exercise. With the best air in the Los Angeles area, cool evening breezes, high-end and varied restaurants, a place for walking or jogging with views of the ocean, and excellent private schools it was a city that only the affluent could afford. All homes were sold in a day or so, usually with a bidding war that made real estate agents happy and frustrated bidders. The less affluent who lived in the city could do so because of a policy of rent control. The mixture of rich and poor, all white, was one of the things Zuma liked about the city. Less likable was the fact that the only people of color that were seen in the city were the gardeners and housekeepers who had traveled in from East L.A. or those housekeepers that lived in the homes of their employers and who walked their children in the morning. The joggers who passed them rarely looked at their faces but would admire and smile at the faces of the white children in their $1,000 strollers. On mornings when Zuma could see passengers getting off, he could imagine the bus had come from Mexico instead of East, L.A. These are the residents he knew that would celebrate Cinco de Mayo by playing Peggy Lees' song that was insulting to people who worked so hard. The song strongly suggests that all problems can wait because time will fix it.

"The window she is broken and the rain is comin' in. If someone doesn't fix it, I'll be soaking to my skin, but if we wait a day or two the rain may go away. And we don't need a window on such a sunny day." (Mañana, mañana, mañana is soon enough for me)

His mind returned to the woman sitting in front of him He wondered if she would celebrate Cinco in that way. He also wondered if Ms. Henderson had children. If she did, he knew she would have those $1,000. strollers. Her presence had made him think of her as a woman who said, 'Here I am; I'm expensive but I'm worth it.' Even if there was a Mr. Henderson, she was not going to change her presentation of herself.

When he arrived, he saw that Henderson and Julian Bateman, the bookman had been put into separate rooms. He brought them into his office along with his chief assistant Zack Caldwell.

"I'm here to hear each of your versions of what is going on. Ms. Henderson feels you are stalking her. I don't want any interruptions. You will each get to refute or rebut anything that the other person has said. Ms. Henderson, why don't you go first."

The woman told the same story that she had told Zuma earlier.

"What is your version of what you are doing Mr. Bateman. I know your name because of the trial that I followed and you were signed in earlier."

"I want to see if she is going to use another designer for her home. So I follow her home in the morning and follow her throughout the day. If she uses another designer, I want a percentage of what the person earns."

"Mr. Bateman I'm not a lawyer but I think you would have trouble winning that case in court."

"I agree Detective. But I think that the case could be embarrassing to this successful realtor as I am seeking work in the city I just moved to."

"Detective, do you see how he can spin his "woe is me, I'm new to the city and looking for work' story". But everyone will know you basically stole money from the woman in line at Barnes and Noble."

"That evidence will not be permitted in court. If they have read about me in the papers, they will not necessarily make the connection. There are no pictures of me in any of the local newspapers."

"I have a proposal that would prevent a messy trial that no one will win. Ms. Henderson would you agree to give Mr. Bateman $500 and in exchange Mr. Bateman would you agree to not bring a lawsuit against Ms. Henderson and she can do whatever she wants to do with your design.?"

Leona Henderson paused. She was not accustomed to losing or compromising. But she was also a smart calculating woman and saw that the $500 would be a small price to pay to get rid of the bookman. "I agree."

"So do I."

Zack, can you please draw up something in the front office. It won't be a legal document but with you witnessing it and my testimony it will stand up in court."

"Sure, Joe."

"You may both leave now."

Zuma felt in his bones that this would not be the end of the bookman. He was a liar and knew how to charm the ladies. Nor did he feel he would never see the lady realtor again. She used any connections she had to promote herself and her business.

# 3

# A Shooter and a Boyfriend

Zuma was right. He saw her but not in the way he expected. Two days after the two parties had signed the agreement, Leona Henderson was shot in front of her home. The gunman had shot her as she was bending down to get her newspaper. The bullet grazed her skull and she fell to the ground. Since she was now a small target the gunman must have not wanted to alert neighbors with a second shot. Zuma knew that the shooter was not that good. He had the scene roped off and had some of the officers going door to door asking neighbors if they had seen or noticed anything about the shooter or the car he had used. Her live-in boyfriend, Richard Boyle, said that he was asleep when he heard the shot but came downstairs when he saw that she was not in bed.

"I looked outside because I didn't see her or the paper and saw her lying on the ground. I went over to her. She was breathing but unconscious. I called 911 and they had an ambulance here in under two minutes."

"Who usually gets the paper, Mr. Boyle?"

"We have no regular routine, detective. Whoever is up first gets the paper and puts on the coffee. Sometimes, she gets it and comes back to bed and I will occasionally do the same."

"Do you own a weapon, Mr. Boyle?"

"Yes, I do. It is locked in a safe that is next to my side of the bed."

"Would you mind going upstairs and opening the safe so I can see your gun?

"Of course not, Detective."

Boyle dropped his jaw when he saw that the safe did not have his gun.

'I don't understand this Detective. Leona and I are the only ones who have the combination aside from our two lawyers."

"And what kind of gun was it and was it registered?"

"I'm not even sure what kind it was I haven't used it in years and of course it is registered."

"Mr. Boyle I am going to ask you not to leave the state or country."

"Why, Detective, you don't think I had anything to do with this shooting?"

"I didn't say you did, but we may need you as the case unfolds, and I want to be able to contact you quickly. I need to have my crew go through the house to search for fingerprints or any other evidence that might prove useful later on. I will tell them to be careful with their belongings. I see that there are a number of expensive paintings and statues."

"Yes, Leona was a collector. She was an art history major at UCLA, years ago."

"I'm going to put a guard in front of her room at the hospital. The guard will alert me when she regains consciousness. I will need to ask her questions. Please don't talk to her before I do. Mr. Boyle do you know anyone who would want to kill Ms. Henderson?"

"I don't know of anyone in particular. Real estate in this town is tough. Some clients or other realtors may have gotten angry with her. Leona was a very sharp person in her business."

"Do you know a Mr. Bateman?"

"Leona told me about this guy who she felt was stalking her and that she was going to meet with you. I offered to go down and speak to the jerk but she felt it was too risky. I saw him standing outside our home a couple of nights."

"Thank you, Mr. Boyle. I'll probably see you in the hospital but please remember that I need to speak with her before you do. Mr. Boyle, could you tell me what business you are in?"

"I'm in the same business as Leona. That is how we met. Of course, I work with a different company. We compete for the same high-end clientele. Most of the time she would win."

"Did this competition make your relationship difficult?"

"No, detective. Leona and I agreed we would never talk about business once we left the office."

Zuma knew that because couples didn't talk about things did not mean there were no strong feelings. In this case, he thought that Boyle as a man might often feel defeated by Leona's winning. Because of possible additional feelings of envy and jealousy, Zuma wondered if Boyle could feel murderous.

# 4

# Friends Who Don't Trust

"Ms. Henderson, I know your uncomfortable and in pain but it's important that you talk to me as soon as possible. Time will make your memory fade. Do you think you can talk now?"

"I'll try detective. Where's my boyfriend?"

"He's outside the door. He is eager to see you. I told him that I had to speak to you first and alone. As soon as we finish, he will be able to come in. Tell me all you can recall. You came out of your house to pick up the newspaper. What do you remember?"

"It wasn't light yet so I can't be too sure, but I thought I saw a man, at least I think it was a man come out from behind a tree. I saw a flash and felt something hit my head. That was the last thing I remember."

"Is there anything else you can recall?"

"No, detective. The next thing I knew is I'm here talking to you."

"You're going to have to leave now detective. We need to check her vitals."

"Thank you, nurse. Please invite the gentleman who is waiting outside when you are through. Can you tell me if Ms. Henderson will be here overnight?"

"It would be quite unusual if the doctor let her go home. She has had a concussion and usually, we require that patients be under observation for 48 hours. If they insist upon leaving, they have to sign a waiver absolving us of any possible damages resulting from the concussion."

"Ms. Henderson, I'll see you when you are safe in the confines of your home. Thank you for your help today. I hope your recovery goes well."

Back at the precinct Zack and Zuma put the names on the board of victims and suspects.

"We got a couple of B & Bs, Joe."

"What do you mean Zack?"

"A bookman and a boyfriend as suspects."

"I see the boyfriend as a possible. He would get rid of serious and successful competition. Let's check to see if she left a will. Maybe there is more for him to gain. The bookman would not have too much to gain except revenge."

"Joe, maybe he was hired by the boyfriend."

"That seems like a long shot to me. He's a liar and a thief of sorts but I don't think he's a murderer. But I have been wrong before. Let's put a tail on both of them. If he was hired, he may want money. If he wasn't, I'm sure we'll find he's up to something."

"Let me be the tail for the bookman. I think he is more than a liar and a thief."

"I'll get someone to tail Boyle and we probably should put someone else in front of the Henderson home. I know you'll already be there but this extra would be in case she leaves."

Two days after Leona Henderson arrived home from the hospital the bookman knocked on her door. She had no trouble letting him in, looking furtively to see if anyone was watching.

"Joe you won't believe it but the man she said she couldn't trust has entered her home and she certainly did not seem frightened or surprised."

"You were right Zack. It seems that he is more than a liar and a thief."

"What do you want me to do, Joe? I could knock on the door and easily confront them."

"No, just record the meeting time on your phone. If he comes out alone continue to follow him. If they come out together try and get a picture and have the other tail and you follow them

Leona Henderson and Julian Bateman left together and went to a pawn shop. Batmen showed a fake ID, Leona paid cash and they left the shop separately. Leona returned home while Zack followed Bateman who went to a shooting range where he practiced for an hour using the weapon he had just acquired.

# 5

# The Rich and Famous

"What could those two be up to? They don't trust or even like each other. What are some possible scenarios?"

"The bookman had a change of heart when he found out she had been shot and decided to return the money."

"So why would they both go to purchase a gun?"

"Maybe he spun a tail that if she was shot, he might be next, and he wanted protection. She felt sorry for him and decided to give him the money for the gun."

"I don't think Leona is the kind of woman who falls for the same sob story two times in a row. I wonder if they are in cahoots in some way?"

"Maybe Leona thought her boyfriend was behind the shooting and decided to hire someone to shoot him when he got the paper in the morning. And maybe the person she hired was our very same bookman."

"But if she hired Bateman, why would he shoot her?"

"The answerer to that might tell us who attempted to kill Leona. We need to check on the boyfriend and see what he might gain if Leona died. We need to get hold of both of their wills. Get a subpoena Zack so we can speak to the lawyers."

"The boyfriends will leave all assets to Leona. There were no children or other relatives listed. Leona will indicate that if the relationship lasted ten years, the boyfriend would get nothing. Paintings and statutes to be turned over to the UCLA Historical Art Society. If the relationship lasted 15 years, the value of all possessions shall be dived equally between the two parties. If the relationship lasted twenty or thirty more years, the boyfriend would get 75 percent of the value of the possessions."

"How many years has the will been in existence?"

"Fourteen."

"So, the boyfriends' motivation to kill her would be diminished if the relationship would end now before the 15th year."

"That's the way I read it also, Zack. On the other hand, her motivation to prevent him from getting anything would be higher. We need to know more about their relationship. Let's start talking to their neighbors, their work colleague's and anyone else whom we think might know them. We also need to keep our tails on all three of them. Zack, can you get a record from her bank on deposits? I know she was successful but those paintings cost a hell of a lot more than she could be making from her real estate sales."

The next two days were relatively uneventful. Leona did not leave the house. Boyle went to work, and the bookman went to the firing range to practice.

"Joe, you're on to something. Her deposits were in two separate saving accounts. One was her business and the other was for a philanthropy account that she would not have to pay taxes for. That showed $20,000 a month for the last two years.

Zuma recalled his comments about Leona. 'I'm high priced but worth it.'

Could she be an expensive call girl? The only other way to get money like that was through the selling of drugs.

"Zack, is there a way to scare some of her clients? Leona will say nothing, but they might turn on her if it would save them the embarrassment of appearing in court about drug use and having their children know anything."

"Good idea, Joe. Let me run with this. I always like to confront the rich and famous. It gives me great pleasure to see that they might be fearful."

Zuma knew that Zack Caldwell had grown up poor and probably suffered in the ways that the poor suffer when they meet with those who are wealthier. Not being looked at. Not being remembered. Forgetting of names.

"Happy that you can do that for me, Zack. Indicate to them the investigation involves drugs and attempted murder. That should scare them more than any drug charges."

The first woman that Zack confronted said that they would not talk unless a lawyer and their husband were present. Zack indicated that he would be happy to wait the rest of the day. It did not take very long for the lawyer or the husband to show up.

When the lawyer asked why their clients were being investigated, Zack told him they were suspects in a drug investigation and a possible murder case."

"And can you show us what evidence you have for either charge?"

"I cannot show you any evidence at this time. We are in the preliminary stages of the investigation."

"I advise you to say nothing until they are prepared to show cause."

"I don't want to wait. I want to say something about drugs."

"I'd advise you again to say absolutely nothing."

"Thank you for your advice counselor. Detective Caldwell, I bought drugs on a regular basis from the realtor that sold me our house."

The husband did not look shocked.

"Could you also say roughly how much you were spending a month?"

"It's hard to say but I'd guess that it was about $2,000.00 a month."

Again, there was no look of surprise on the husbands' face.

"Because of your cooperation, I'm sure the DA will look favorably on your case. You are allowed to purchase drugs in this state but have to do so legally. Yours was an illegal purchase. I will make sure to indicate you cooperated."

"Thank you."

Zack got two more women who went through the same routine. He suspected that the first one had called her friends to tell them would be better off if they cooperated. He left feeling good about confronting and exposing the rich and famous with their secrets.

# 6

# Sting Like a Bee

"Zack, this is what I think we've got. A fancy realtor selling drugs to her fancy counterparts in Santa Monica; a bookman trying to improve his shooting skills and a live-in boyfriend who didn't want to have his girlfriend break up in the next month because he will lose a lot of cash. What did you find from the neighbors?"

"Joe, this very happy couple had lots of screaming matches. The neighbors had to call the police a few times because they were worried. I checked the police blotter and no charges were filed except 'domestic disturbance.'"

The call came in from the tail who was supposed to be watching Boyle.

"Chief, I'm sorry I got here a few minutes late but Richard Boyle was shot. I went up to the body and he was barely breathing and unconscious. I called the ambulance. The medics were not sure he is going to make it."

"I'm going to have to put this in your file Ralston.

"Of course, I understand chief. I'm sorry I screwed up."

"Meet me at the hospital, Ralston."

Zack and Zuma didn't have to wonder who would benefit from Boyle's death.

"Ralston, what else do you remember about the scene? Did you see any neighbors come out? Did any of them notice a car? Were there footprints? It had rained the night before."

"I screwed up, Chief, but I think I did everything else right. One neighbor saw a black car with no plate that he could recognize. I did get footprints. I also taped the area and we're getting a picture of the prints. I need to go back and ask the neighbor what make car he thought it might be."

"You stay here. You did well after the screw-up, but we want you to stay here. The neighbor might be more relaxed with a new face. The footprints will tell us something about the weight of the shooter. Call me if he gains consciousness. Do not let anyone else in. We're going to have to pay a visit to our now familiar suspects."

"Thank you, Chief. I will call you immediately if there is any change."

The suspects had alibis for the time of the shooting. Leona was picking up the paper and a neighbor had spotted her and they started chatting. The neighbor was glad that Leona was back from the hospital. The bookman was at his usual place having coffee at Starbucks. The clerks knew him and he could easily get one to vouch for him and he also had a receipt for his coffee and danish.

The weight of the shooter was estimated to be over 200 pounds. It could not have been the realtor or the bookman.

"Zack, lets' go home and start afresh tomorrow. I need a break and it would be good for me to have dinner with Claudia."

Over dinner, Zuma expressed his frustration with the case.

"I want a simple murder case. Just one based on sex, drugs, or money. These rich people have all kinds of motives and they twist and turn and switch. back. They remind me of Muhammed Ali. There is all this twisting and turning and dancing about just like Ali could when he wanted to be the butterfly."

Claudia laughed. "Joe, you have told me that no case is simple. This one just seems more difficult because of the duplicity. I am sure that you, in time, will be able to figure it out even it is more difficult than most. And when that time comes, you will sting like a bee."

# 7

# Who Shall Benefit?

"The shooter was over 200 pounds so that could not be our realtor or bookman."

"Clearly Leona would benefit if the boyfriend was killed before the 15th year. Zack, I don't see any benefit for our bookman."

"Maybe she hired someone else, Joe?"

"That's a possibility. Can we check her phone to see the calls she has made in the past few weeks?"

"I'll do that."

"Who else might gain from the boyfriends' death?"

"Maybe we need to not think of gain but of jealousy or revenge"

"That would involve any of the men that Leona met and there were many from the husbands of the wives she was dealing drugs to and others."

"I think we have to go back and ask those wives if they have noticed anything unusual in their husbands' behavior in the past few months."

The first wife that Zack called upon was completely surprised. She was quick to indicate that she had already spoken to the police and had cooperated reporting her drug use and it seemed that a settlement had been agreed to. She also reported that there did not seem to be anything unusual in his behavior. Other than his forgetting to pick things up on the way home a little more often, his patterns seem to be the same. The second wife seemed to be expecting the visit, so Zack assumed that wife number one had called ahead.

"I have already cooperated with the police and I will not answer any questions you have about my husbands' behavior."

"I guess I will have to call you both in since this investigation involves a murder, not just drug usage."

"Feel free to do whatever you need to do, detective. We have nothing to hide."

The last sentence was a giveaway for Zack. How would she know 'they' would have nothing to hide unless she had already spoken to the girlfriend who had mentioned drug usage?

He decided to call them in and to get a warrant to inspect both of their phones and their computers.

"I can cuff you both and drag you down to the precinct or I can trust you to get there on your own. You can also make your phone call to your lawyer so he can meet you."

"Thank you, detective. We will meet you there."

The moment Zuma left and was out of earshot the wife started to scream.

"You are a first-class jerk. I told you to cut it off and that it was dangerous to continue. I could put up with your affairs, but I will not cover for you in any way if you are involved with this murder. If you are, this may be a lucky break for me. I won't have to put up with your crap and the constant lying anymore."

Zack told Zuma about the warrants that he would need and that the two of them were coming in and would probably have their lawyer. When the Bosworth's arrived, it was clearly visible they were agitated and must have been arguing. Their lawyer asked for the charges and the reply was for the investigation of a murder. When he asked for the evidence, Zuma said that evidence was in the process of being gathered. The lawyer requested that his clients be let go until such evidence was gathered.

"Officers, my husband has had affairs over the years. I am sick of his behavior. I know nothing about a murder."

"Do you know any of the women he has had affairs with, especially the most recent one?"

"You'll have to ask him."

"I have nothing to say at this time, detectives."

The warrants obtained evidence that there had been a lot of phone calls to Leona and to the boyfriend.

# Excellent Liars

"Detectives, phone calls between my client, Brian Bosworth, and these two other people are not evidence of murder. I insist he be released immediately."

"It's alright I am willing to talk. Here's my story, detectives, I was and still am in love with Leona and I was jealous of the damn boyfriend. I told Leona that I was planning to leave my wife. She told me not to bother. She was not interested in seeing me anymore. I was devastated. But I am not a murderer."

"Why did you call the boyfriend?"

"I was hoping he would leave. I told him stupid things like Leona was breaking up with him and that I was the one she wanted to be with."

"What was his reaction to these 'stupid things'?"

"I think he got scared. I knew about the 14-year arrangement that he and Leona had. So, I think he must have thought that I was after him."

"Did Leona Henderson hire you to shoot the live-in?"

"I told you, detectives; I am a liar, but I am not a murderer."

Zuma and Zack began laughing

"Forgive us for laughing. But you have to admit that it's pretty funny that right after you admit that you're a liar you say you are not a murderer."

"I guess that does sound stupid and ridiculous."

"Mr. Bosworth, we are going to ask for your passport. I strongly urge you not to make any kinds of travel plans. We will need you to stay close in case any new evidence crops up."

"I guess it would be silly to repeat that I am not a murderer."

"You are welcome to repeat it as often as you like. We can repeat that you told us that you are a liar. You can leave now."

"That was fun, Joe."

"I enjoyed the repartee also. I'm sure it registered with you Zack that he weighs over two hundred but we are no further ahead in the case. I think we have to go back and pay Leona Henderson a visit. We may have to do a little fabricating of our own."

"Ms. Henderson, one of your client's husband says that he was in love with you and that you suggested he should get rid of your boyfriend so that the two of you could be together. He also said that you would be willing to pay him some money if the 14-year arrangement was not fulfilled. He also said that you told him the date that it should be done by."

"Well, you know the man is a very good liar. He was able to lie for years about his affairs."

"Yes, we are aware that he is a liar. He in fact told us that. The question for you is, did you do any of the things he says you did?"

"Absolutely not."

"Thank you, Ms. Henderson. I will ask you for your passport and urge you not to make any travel plans. We may need you as a witness as the case moves forward."

"Joe, I think we are dealing with two very excellent liars."

"You are very right Zack."

Two days later, one of the very excellent liars was killed.

# 9

# The Buyer and the Seller

Brian Bosworth was found shot to death outside his home. He was in a jogging outfit and probably getting ready for a morning run. His running shoes matched the footprints that had been left in the mud outside the bookman's apartment.

"That's one way to get rid of a suspect.

I'm not sure if it will add another one to our list or if we just stay with the two, we already have. Joe, I think it is time for another visit to our other very excellent liar.?

I have another idea, Zack. The income she was generating from her selling of drugs would not have covered the costs of those paintings. Maybe she has another source of income that she has not told us about. I'm going to ask her if she would be willing to sell any of them. I'll say I have a buyer. I'll invite Claudia to examine them. I can be an excellent liar if I have to."

Leona was happy to be told about the potential buyer. She said very little as she showed Claudia around. After looking at 12 of them Claudia asked the prices for three of them.

"I'm glad you like those. Those are my favorites at this point. Do you recognize the paintings and the painter?"

"Yes, I do."

Leona handed her separate slips with the names of the painter, the painting and the price.

"I will also be able to provide you with documentation of prior sellers of the paintings, the prices they received, and a certificate of authenticity."

"Thank you, Ms. Henderson. My accountant will be getting back to you." The moment she left Leona's home she called Joe.

"Joe, the paintings are absolutely fraudulent. They are good imitations but not genuine. She sells them to buyers and provides them with a phony certificate of authenticity."

"Claudia, what's your experience or knowledge with cases like this?"

"I have no direct experience but people who get caught are put on a list that all agents who are searching for paintings can refer to. Also, it is criminal to misrepresent but I'm not sure what happens. They can get probably get time off if they give the money back. I think the paintings are confiscated."

"Claudia, you just helped me think of the trap that we will use on Ms. Henderson."

Claudia made the call.

"I am definitely want to buy one of the three paintings. I will think about the other two. Do you think you can hold on to the other two for a month?

"That won't be a problem. When can I expect your check?"

"I can bring it over today and would like to pick up the painting. Can you trust me? You can call my bank to see if the check is covered. I live locally and will not skip town with the work. If you don't want a check, I can have my bank wire the funds to your bank but that will take at least two days. The check will be for sixty-eight thousand dollars. Is that correct?"

"Yes, it is. I prefer a check rather than a wire transfer. What time can I expect you?"

"I'll go with you Claudia. She'll let you in. If she sees me, she might refuse entrance. I want this to go as smoothly as possible. Can you tell me how she goes about acquiring those phony paintings?"

"There are artists who have not been successful and can't make a living but who are very good at imitating. What they can't imitate is the kind of oils that were used in the old days. Time does something to them that makes it impossible to replicate. The oils gave it away. That's how I knew they were absolutely fraudulent."

"Fraudulent, my dear Claudia, is something you have never been."

# 10

# Verifying Authenticity

"We need to get a warrant to collect all the paintings she has in her house. She has probably been selling them to her clients along with the drugs."

"We'll need to collect them as well but let's wait 'till we book her."

Zuma called Zack and said he would wait for him as he wanted to have the house in lockdown after Leona was booked.

"Joe it's not clear to me what the benefits of getting her on charges of fraud will be. It's a civil offense not criminal."

"I know, Zack, I don't think it will lead her to a confession of murder if that is what she did. I could see how she might confess if she gets a reduced sentence and gives all the money back and hopes that her cooperation will be looked upon favorably by the court. She might also mount a strong case of self-defense."

Leona Henderson opened the door after looking through the peephole and saw that it was Claudia. She dropped her jaw when she saw that Zuma and his associate were behind her.

"Sorry to disappoint you, Ms. Henderson. The art buyer recognized the three pieces she selected as fraudulent and we wonder if you are aware of that? We also wonder if the other works you have are fraudulent?"

"No, of course not. Why would I purchase fraudulent art? I was an art history major at UCLA, one of the finest programs in the country and I love art and I love collecting. And I love putting good art into people's homes."

"And you love making money by doing that, correct?

"Of course I do. There is nothing wrong with making money and it makes me feel good that I am bringing something beautiful into their lives."

"I guess it goes well with the drugs you also brought into their lives."

"Detectives, if you are going to book me, I need to call my lawyer."

While Leona Henderson was taken to the precinct, Zuma told his staff that they need to gather evidence that the other paintings were also frauds. He told his officers that they needed first to ask for the paintings and if they refused had they would get a warrant. If they give you the paintings give them a receipt. Tell them there is a good possibility that their money will be refunded. Make sure they know they have to be very careful in handling the paintings."

"Detective, are you going to bring the same charges as earlier?"

"No, this is not a criminal charge. This involves knowingly selling of art under false pretenses by providing phony certificates of authenticity."

"And how do you propose to establish that my client knowingly did that? She was a serious student of art so why would she spend her money to purchase paintings that were fraudulent?"

"For the simple reason that she could sell them. At this very moment, we are collecting the works that we believe were sold to her clients."

The lawyer advised Leona that she need not say anything further.

"I'm not worried. I had the certificate verifying the authenticity of the work and had no reason to doubt it. I will testify in court that I believed I was purchasing the genuine, original piece of work. Moreover, I would be willing to reimburse all buyers their original price plus interest. I will take the loss for being played by some dealer."

Zuma smiled. It was the way he had predicted she would react to the charges saying the exact words he had said. The woman was strong and he thought of the lyrics to the Tom Petty, song. "I Won't Back Down."

'I won't back down.

Stand me up at the gates of hell.

But I won't back down.

No, I'll stand my ground. Won't be turned around.

"Joe, we're just going around in circles. We're no closer to figuring out this murder case than we were before."

"I know Zack. I'm dizzy from all of it.

"Let's meet in the morning, Joe. Hopefully, a good night's sleep will clear my head."

# 11

# A Strong and Clever Wife

"You're going to tell that woman you are through with her. And I'm going to go with you to make sure."

"And what if I refuse?"

"If you are not prepared to do this I will seek a divorce immediately with full custody and tell the children about all the affairs you have been having. I don't think that our kids or your fellow salesmen will look too kindly upon you."

Leona opened the door and smiled until she saw the wife behind her boyfriend.

"Tell her."

"I can't."

"Then I will. He is through with you. Your relationship is done with. It is over and now it is really over."

Allison Stuart pulled out a revolver from her purse and shot Leona Henderson in the heart.

"My god how could you do that?"

"I could do that and I'm going to do more" At which point she walked up to her husband as if she was going to kiss him. He was surprised but his mouth was awaiting her kiss. Instead, he felt the coolness of the steel and that was the last sensation he felt. She wiped off the weapon, stuck it in his hand so it would have his fingerprints, and left it next to his body. She looked at the two bodies and admired the way she had planned and pulled this off. She picked up her cell.

"Police? I want to report what looks like murder or suicide. There are two bodies I have discovered. Yes, I will wait for you to arrive. Here is the address."

When Zuma and Zack arrived, they found Allison Stuart sitting on a bench sobbing. Zuma spoke.

"Mrs. Stuart, I know this is a difficult time for you but can you tell us how you came to be in Leona Henderson's home?"

"We were at home and I had decided I had enough of his affairs and his promises to break up with this woman. Told him he had to do or I would divorce him, seek custody of the children and let the world know about his many affairs. He said he would do it but I didn't trust him so I followed her. I was expecting to hear screaming, shouting, and crying. Instead, I heard what I assumed to be two gunshots. I became scared but the door was open so I entered. then saw the two of them on the floor with the gun next to my husband's body."

Did you check to see if there was a pulse or any breathing?"

I didn't. I think I was in shock and the only thing I could think of was calling the police."

Zuma believed the woman was lying while also admiring, what he believed to be, the ingenuity of her plan. He hesitated to bring up his request knowing how most women would respond.

"Mrs. Stuart, I am going to give you my jacket so that you can remove your blouse. Please go into the bathroom and return with the blouse. My jacket will cover you."

"Detective Zuma this is outrageous. Are you hitting on me? This is sexual harassment. I want to call another police officer."

"Number one, I am not hitting on you. Number two, you are welcome to call another police officer. The officer, when he arrives, will tell you this is standard procedure. This will also take some time while we both sit here with the two corpses."

Allison Stuart knew that Zuma must have some good reason for his asking her to get the blouse to him. She thought it better to cooperate than to resist since she would have to do it later. She even thought a lawyer could not prevent the request since this was the required protocol. When she got into the bathroom the only thing, she could imagine doing with her bouse was to shake it out not even understanding why she was doing this.

She emerged covered in Zuma's jacket.

"Thank you, Mrs. Stuart. I want to make sure about any fingerprints. Did you touch anything else in the room? I assume your fingerprints will be on your blouse and your cellphone"

"No, I touched nothing. I'm beginning to shiver may I go home now?

Office Caldwell will drive you home. He will be asking for your passport. Please give it to him. I will return your blouse after we have had a chance to do some laboratory work with it."

"Why do you need my passport"

"Because I believe I will be arresting you for the murder of your husband and Leona Henderson."

"You are out of your mind detective. I told you exactly what happened. I'm sure there will be no fingerprints on the gun."

"I'm sure of that also. But the evidence will probably be in your blouse."

"Now I know you're losing your mind."

"You might be right, Mrs. Allison but the evidence does not lie. We will see what our lab discovers."

For the first time, Allison Stuart felt fear. She knew how to cover it up.

"I'm getting colder and I need to call my lawyer."

"Joe, I think we just found another excellent liar."

# 12

# Harassment

The lawyer was at the precinct waiting for Zack Caldwell to bring his client in. When they arrived, the lawyer began talking immediately.

"I think this is an outrageous detective. I believe we may have a case for sexual harassment. What possible grounds would you have to ask my client to remove her clothes."

"Slow down counselor. I did not ask Mrs. Stuart to remove her clothes. I asked her to remove her blouse. I gave her a jacket to protect her and to preserve any modesty she might feel. In a shooting when people are close to each other, it is police protocol to ask for items of clothing. I had reason to believe that this was not a murder suicide. I would present whatever evidence we can establish from the blouse at a trial if this is where we are going.

"Let me confer in private with my client." Zuma and Zack left the room.

"Allison. I know Zuma. When he goes to the DA it's usually b because he's got solid evidence and he most frequently gets a conviction from the DA s office. You need to tell me the truth. That is the only way I can help you."

Allison starts sobbing but also admits to the murders.

"O.K. This is what we are going to do. You are going to go back in there and tell them you did it. If they want to take you to trial, we will make a case that you were an embittered wife, frustrated by years of affairs and that you wanted to have your marriage back. There is no evidence that the gun was yours. You can argue that your husband went in with a gun and flew into a fit of rage when he was turned down and killed her. You grabbed the gun trying to wrestle it from him. You tried to show him you still loved him by kissing him. When he opened his mouth, you were still trying to take the gun away and it went off."

Allison continued to sob but nodded her head.

"Detective my client is ready to tell you what happened. She will be pleading guilty. You can book her now. I will post bail. You have her passport so she will not be able to flee the country."

"Joe, we need to sit down. We just solved two murders and will probably get the murderer put away. But there are other things that are still going on."

"I know Zack. When they leave let's sit down and put our heads together. No phone calls, until we figure out what we go and where we can go from here. I think Leona Henderson started this and I still feel she is the key."

# 13

# Circles

"Joe, we have Leona Henderson selling drugs and fraudulent paintings. She has also been shot. We have Julian Bateman, a liar, who seems to be connected to Leona. We have Leona's boyfriend Richard Boyle who also has been shot. We have a husband, Brian Bosworth, shot to death by his wife. We have Allison Stuart who also shot her husband."

Zuma started humming.,

"I don't recognize that one Joe. Can you sing me the words?"

"It's an oldie by Joni Mitchell and it's called "The Circle Game." Here are some of the words:

>And the seasons they go round and round
>And the painted ponies go up and down
>We're captive on the carousel of time
>We can't return we can only look behind
>From where we came
>And go round and round and round
>In the circle game."

"That a very appropriate depiction of this case. I do feel like we are going round and round and up and down."

"OK. Instead of going round and round let's get back on the ground. I think Leona Henderson started all this and I think she is the key. Can you check those bank account deposits again and see if she has been declaring them on her taxes? I know she will be very worried if the US treasury finds out she has been hiding income. You'll need a new warrant to let the bank show you the information."

Zuma started humming again.

"Joe, this is my lucky day I get to learn two new songs. What's this one?"

"The words don't apply Zack but the title does. It's called "What's Going On." It's a great song made famous by a great singer, Marvin Gaye but only the title applies to what we are trying to do right now."

"I'll make it my business to listen, Joe. Thanks for the two recommendations."

# 14

# Creating a New Business

"Leona, I'm glad I caught you in. This is Pamela Langston. I have a proposal and it's one that I don't think you can or should refuse. I have been buying drugs from you for three years and have spent close to a total of 75 thousand dollars. I have also brought three paintings from you and spent 75 thousand on each. So, I've given you about three hundred thousand over the past few years. I've always paid you on time and never argued or haggled with you about prices"

"Where is this going? I don't hear any proposal"

"You know I own a fancy hair salon. Women with lots of money come in and want the full works: Manicure, Pedicure, Hair coloring, and Massage. They are always looking for bargains. Here's the deal l can offer them. I will sell your paintings to them. I don't think they give a damn about the paintings they are buying. They just want to show off and it will be easy for them to brag when they can show the letter of authenticity. The letter will allow them to deal with anyone who doubts the value of the paintings they purchase. I have over 100 clients. If I sell only twenty of them, at a cost of 75,000 each, we earn two and one half million dollars. That's a million and a quarter for each of us. I know I am not including your expenses but I think it could be very lucrative for each of us. And that is only if we sell twenty paintings. I'm sure once the others hear about the bargain, we can sell a lot more. I can also tell them about drugs at a bargain price and one that is safe from being discovered and you can keep all that money to yourself. How can you refuse this?"

Leona was unsure. She was happy with the way things had been. Would it be risky to enlarge her business now? She thought Zuma was already very suspicious of her and wanted to get something oh her that was more than a civil offense. On the other hand, she was a shrewd businesswoman. She would have a record of all the paintings and drugs that were given to Pamela. The idea that new sales of drugs with all profits going to her was appealing and generous. She began fantasizing about earning two or three million a year but caught herself. She knew it was dangerous as a business person to count the chickens before they hatched.

"Pamela, thank you for your generosity about my possible drug selling. Let's start slowly. I will have to contact the persons I buy from. It will take about two weeks before I have some paintings to give you. You can count on having five to start with. As business people, we know it is wise to start slowly. You and I know we can't always anticipate everything. Can you tell me why you are looking to expand?"

"Like you, Leona, I'm a business person and I'm always looking for ways to increase my income."

When Leona got off the phone, she immediately made five phone calls. She did not want to give all the business to one person. Someone might get suspicious about all the mailings if they were done by any one person. She decided to let another five of her contacts be ready for an increase in business. She was anticipating that this might be a very busy time for her having to make so many different phone calls but it could be well worth it as it seemed like it might turn out to be an extremely lucrative arrangement. She started to fantasize again, about early retirement and devoting herself exclusively to collecting authentic art, but stopped herself

# 15

# The Guilty Benefit

Leona Henderson was surprised when she saw the two detectives at her front door.

"I've been advised by consul not to talk to any officers of the law unless she is present."

"You don't have to say a word, Ms. Henderson. We can do all the talking and it will be brief. We just had your IRS payments checked and it looks like you did not declare the income from your drug selling and your philanthropies to the feds. That is all we wanted to tell you. We are sure you would want to know what we have been doing and have found out."

Leona's first thought was that she could pay off the feds what she owed including any penalty. Her second thought was that she had better hold off on setting up the arrangement with Pamela until everything with the feds was settled. This was not going to stop her.

"Thank you, detectives. Can we arrange a meeting with my consul?"

"That would be fine. I want this done at the precinct. Do you want to call her now?"

"Yes. Can I drive or do you want me to go in the car with you?"

"Please come with us. Your consul will be able to take you back."

"My client is prepared to pay all monies due to the IRS plus whatever penalties might have accrued."

"We're glad to hear that. It will save your client lots of money if she went to trial. Is there anything else your client would be willing to do? Like would she be willing to stop collecting phony art"

The attorney looked at Leona who nodded no and spoke.

"I can never be sure detectives if the art is phony detectives. If I get a letter verifying its authenticity, that's good enough for me."

"My client wants to continue to invest in art, detectives. Surely, that is not against the law."

"You're right consul. It's against the law to not pay taxes on income and to knowingly sell items that claim to be genuine but which she knows to be phony. And forgive my sarcasm counsel but these are things she never would have reported unless they were discovered. Luckily, she can now appear to be an upright citizen by paying back taxes and fines and claiming either ignorance or blaming her accountant. It will probably get her more real estate clients when she claims she has been pursued by the IRS. It's a great country isn't it counsel when a guilty person can benefit?"

# 16

# George Gershwin

"Claudia, I need to talk. I can't even think of a song that might apply to this merry-go-round, loop dee loop we're in. A person is guilty and benefits; a man is murdered because one of my men is late showing up; a man is murdered by his wife who is going to plead not guilty because she was trying to show her affection, and a boyfriend's weapon is missing and he claims he doesn't know how it disappeared"

"Joe, darling I know this is making you dizzy and driving you a bit crazy because you have repeated this before."

"Sorry, Claudia. I guess I am a bit nuts right now. Maybe by the time I see you tonight, it will be better."

The call came in. It made him more nuts but he knew he had to do something even if it was the usual response that he always made when a murder was reported.

"Captain Zuma, Leona Henderson has just been found dead. She was lying in front of her home shot in the heart."

Zuma thought she will never see the benefits that he believed she might get if there was a trial. One less piece of the puzzle to delete and another to add. Who might be responsible? He called Zack and asked him to meet him at the murder scene. He also called Claudia and told her he was less crazy because he had something new to focus upon.

"I knew it, Joe. You just have to learn to be patient. I will have your favorite food ready for you when you get home tonight."

"Good advice, Good food, and a great wife. Who could ask for anything more?"

"And there's your song Joe. I'm sure you remember it. It's that wonderful oldie by George Gershwin."

"As I just said, who could ask for anything more."

# 17

# A Dead End

The crime scene had been roped off. It looked like Leon Henderson was shot as she was picking up the paper. It must have been early in the morning. The same scenario as last time only this time the result was not a concussion but death.

"Zack please be responsible for gathering any evidence. Figure out where the bullet was fired from, the kind of weapon that was used, and footprints. I know I'm repeating myself so forgive me. I know you would do all these things even if I said nothing.

"No problem Joe. We're all under the strain of this dizzy case."

"It's getting dizzier, Zack. Who would benefit from Henderson's death? The boyfriend is dead. There are no heirs. Batemen is not someone she would leave any money for. Maybe he was thinking she was using his designs? And we can't forget that he was practicing and learning to shoot at the shooting range. Maybe he never forgave her even though they seemed to have become buddies."

"But we've been tailing her and we know she hasn't gone to any designers. Bateman is the only one left on this case. Other than him it seems like we're out of suspects."

"Maybe this is the beginning of an entirely new case. Henderson was an ambitious person and maybe she got into something else besides drugs and art?"

"Or maybe she figured a new way to do the art and drug business of hers."

"I'm sure if you check her phone there will be no record of calls made to new persons. She was too smart to leave a record of that."

"Are we stuck? is this a dead-end for us? I'm not sure what else we can do."

"I'm not either Zack. But I'm remembering Claudia's advice to be patient."

# 18

# Another Art Collector

Their patience was rewarded. It took two weeks when a man showed up at the precinct asking to speak to Zuma.

"Detective Zuma I wanted to speak to you directly. I have seen you on TV and know you have been connected to phone art deals. My name is Julius Taylor. I am a businessman but I also do serious art collecting. My wife just brought home a painting and she proudly showed me the letter of authenticity, But I know it is fake. Before I said anything to her, I wanted to speak to you. What do you suggest I do?

"Thank you, Mr. Taylor. You did the right thing. I'd like my assistant to join us, you and I go to your home so we can all speak to your wife. Would that be OK with you? I prefer you don't call her so she can't prepare a story.

"That would be fine. I know she is naive and innocent about this purchase. I don't want to hurt her feelings or make her feel foolish."

"We can make sure of that, Mr. Taylor."

"Honey I brought these two nice officers in because I think there might be a problem with the painting you bought."

"How could there be a problem" I showed you the letter that verifies its authenticity."

"Mrs. Taylor, people who deal in phony art are very clever. You are not the first one to be taken in with a phony letter and a nonauthentic painting. This is not your fault or even your responsibility. We might be able to get your money back, but we need your cooperation. Can you tell us who you purchased the piece from and how much you paid?"

"I purchased it from my hairdresser. I thought it a bit odd but she explained that she was trying to start a new business. I paid one hundred and fifty thousand. She said it would be worth three hundred thousand in two years and said if it wasn't, she would buy it back from me."

"I'm sure she didn't give you a letter indicating that she would do that. Am I correct Mrs. Taylor?'

"No, she didn't. I have been a regular customer for a number of years and I trusted her completely. Her name is Pamela Langston"

"Thank you Mrs. Taylor You have been most helpful. I am going to give you a receipt for this phony painting. We may need it as evidence. Do you have any proof of your purchase?"

"No. She did not want a check so I went to the bank to get cash. You can check for the amount I withdrew. It was exactly the fee for the painting. Julius, I hope none of this is embarrassing to you."

"None of this is. You were fooled by a very smart thief who was an excellent liar. This happens to lots of people."

# 19

# Cooperation

Pamela Langston was blowing out a client's hair when she saw the detectives enter her salon, she knew immediately that they must have found something out. She was hoping that it was just about her art business.

She excused herself to the client and asked an assistant to finish up the job. She then motioned to the detectives to come back into her office.

"Ms. Langston, we just left Mrs. Taylors' home and she showed us a painting you sold her along with the letter you gave to her. We now have the painting as well as evidence that she withdrew the exact fee that you were charging. Would you like to say anything now or we can take you down to the precinct where you can have your lawyer?"

Pamela knew the evidence was solid but she thought she would be in a stronger position if she had a lawyer representing her.

"Let me tell the girls I won't be back and they are to close the shop when they are finished. I'll call my lawyer now."

"My client is willing to admit she sold the painting to Mrs. Taylor but did not know it was a fake."

"We think your client is running a business and selling other paintings. We are going to get a list of all her clients and call them about any possible purchases."

"She still may not have known they were fakes."

"Ms. Langston, would you be willing to give us the name of the dealer or painter whom you bought the paintings from?"

"Pamela, I urge you not to answer."

"I have no problem with that Larry. Here is his name and number." When you call him tell him I referred you."

Pamela Langston felt good. If they called the painter, they would never know about the others that she had purchase paintings from. If they discovered other paintings in her client's homes, she would say that she couldn't ask the painter to deliver that many works in a short period of time.

"Detectives, I want you to know I am an honest person. I am willing to give the money back to Mrs. Taylor plus anything she would want for hurt feelings."

"She seemed very cooperative Joe."

"I know Zack. That degree of cooperation, to me, usually means there is something else the suspect is hiding from us."

"Leona was the person whom she may have had contact but she is dead."

"Zack, please get someone from our shop to call all of Langston's clients about art purchases. Tell them they should say to the client this is part of a murder investigation. We don't want them all calling Langston if they get panicky."

The calls came up with four art purchases. When they told Langston about this discovery, she said that there were some other painters that she dealt with. She willingly gave Zuma the names. She was still feeling good about what she was hiding from Zuma.

"And did you report all this income to the IRS?"

That did not upset or frighten Pamela Langston. She could pay that back also. There was only one thing she was afraid of Zuma becoming suspicious about.

"Zack, let's assume for the moment that Langston and Henderson were in cahoots with each other and Langston for some reason killed or hired someone to kill Leona Henderson. How could we go about proving that?"

"As you said earlier there would be no traces of phone calls. They must have met to plan or to give monies that were being earned. We need to find someone who knows they met or were meeting on some kind of regular basis."

# 20

# A New Excellent Liar

The call came into Zuma as he was driving to work.

"Chief, Julian Bateman was found shot to death in front of a coffee shop early this morning. I didn't want to wake you. I have the place cordoned off."

"I'll be there with Zack in twenty minutes. Keep all the people in the immediate area from leaving. Never be afraid of waking me. This is a 24/7 job for all of us."

"I can't believe it, Joe. No one is left from the original case. Henderson, Boyle, and now Bateman were all shot to death. That's an original way to close a case."

"I don't think the case is closed, Zack. I think of it as continuing. We need to be watching Langston very, very carefully."

The surveillance paid off. An unknown male who entered her home was identified as a suspect for another shooting. He had been let off because the witness had been killed. Zuma had him picked up and had Langston and the suspect in front of him.

"Ms. Langson, Mr. Feller, you are both here because we believe the two of you planned the murder of Julian Bateman. Mr. Feller, you may turned out to be a good fella by keeping your mouth shut or you may turn out to be the fall guy."

Langston's consul spoke.

Detective Zuma, what is your evidence that these two planned, plotted, or executed Mr. Bateman?"

"We want to be, frank consul. There is no direct evidence. We only know that your client was visited by a man who has a criminal record and who has been known to shoot people. He got off a case because the witness was murdered. Why would a legitimate business person want to be dealing with him.? Oh, I forgot. Ms. Langston is not always doing legitimate business. Forgive my sarcasm."

The criminal was clearly not going to say anything. He was waiting to see what Langston would say. After a long silence. She spoke.

"I did not hire this man to kill Bateman. I needed some protection and paid him for his services. Someone had been coming around my house and I was afraid of a break-in and worse."

"Why would you hire a criminal? A legitimate security service would have done the job."

"I have no faith that those people would stand up to a real break-in artist."

"How did you find him?"

"I asked around. Many of the business people I know need security."

"Can you tell us from whom you were given his name?"

"I can't remember Detective."

"The lady speaks the truth, detectives. She paid me and I was working for her for four nights before you hauled my ass in here. I'd like to go now."

"So would I, detectives."

"I'd like to do that but there is another piece of evidence that links you to this murder, Ms. Langston. The bullet casing that was found at Batemans' body was traced to a weapon that Leona Henderson's husband owned. You are the one who had access to that weapon. Maybe he even gave it to you.

We don't think you know how to handle a weapon but we know Mr. Feller knows how to shoot and shoots well. Bateman was killed with one bullet."

Pamela began calculating. If she admitted to giving the gun to Feller, he would deny using it. The gun was the only item linking her indirectly to Batemans' murder.

"I have no knowledge of the gun you are talking about. I know nothing about guns."

"But we found your fingerprints on the gun that was used to kill Bateman."

Zack dropped his jaw. He knew Zuma was making that up. Langston was quick to respond.

"All right, detectives, I did have the gun and I did give it to Mr. Feller, but I did not shoot Bateman."

"We will see if a jury believes that a gun that had been fired with only your fingerprints on it will get you off."

"We are booking you for the murder of Julian Bateman."

As she was led away to be booked, Zuma heard her whisper to Feller.

"You bastard you didn't wipe my prints off as I had asked you to do. You wiped your prints off but left mine."

Upon hearing those words, Zuma approached Feller.

"Mr. Feller, you are under arrest. I am booking you for the murder of Julian Bateman and I will change the charges against Ms. Langston to aiding and abetting a murder. I must warn you that anything you say now may be held against you in court."

"That bitch, I knew she would never be able to keep her mouth shut. I could have testified that her prints were on the gun because she wanted me to own it. She isn't as smart as she thinks she is."

Zuma liked that what Feller had just said could be used in court.

"Joe, that was a shrewd ploy on your part."

"Zack, you never know who can turn out to be an excellent liar."

# 21

# Dining and Celebrating

Zack, Claudia, and Joe were celebrating the closing of the case at Maradentros, a Mexican restaurant located at the corner of Wilshire Boulevard and Barrington Avenue. They were famous for their guacamole. They arrived late so had no trouble getting seated.

"Claudia this case involved four murders, done by three separate murderers, drug selling, and fake art sales."

"I think this is the biggest case you have ever had, Joe. What happened to the fake art painters?"

"They are out of our jurisdiction but I have reported them to the Philadelphia police. I told them to get back to me if they found out anything."

"Can anyone come up with a song that might apply to this case before we finish this delicious guacamole and order?"

Zack spoke. "If I said yes, I would be a liar and probably not an excellent one. I pass."

"Joe. I don't know a song either but there is a phrase from a song that applies to you."

"Which one, Claudia?"

It's the one that Janis Joplin made so famous. I know you know the song. It's "Me and Bobb McGee." But the line that you may not remember goes like this.

"We sang every song that driver knew."

I can substitute the words "I was holding bobby's hand in mine" for your holding my hand in yours. You have been our driver Joe and we love being along for the ride.

"Claudia, thank you for reminding me of that great song. I think I have sung every song I ever knew to you. And I know there's probably one for every occasion."

"Knowing you, Joe, I'm sure there is. And I know you're not lying now."

"Okay. Here's one the seems to fit:

> Happy days are here again
> The skies above are clear again
> So, let's sing a song of cheer again
> Happy days are here again."

"No one can make up an excellent lie about how good this guacamole is. So let's order. I don't think we can go wrong with anything on the menu. Let me order drinks before we order, and thank you both for your help and being with me on this ride and to all the future ones that we shall be taking."

www.ingramcontent.com/pod-product-compliance
Lightning Source LLC
Chambersburg PA
CBHW021451070526
44577CB00002B/365